THE GREAT PIRATE ACTIVITY BOOK

DERI ROBINS

ILLUSTRATED BY GEORGE BUCHANAN

Kingfisher

KINGFISHER
An imprint of Larousse plc
Elsley House, 24-30 Great Titchfield Street, London W1P 7AD

First published in paperback by Kingfisher 1996
2 4 6 8 10 9 7 5 3
Originally published in hardback by Kingfisher 1994

Text copyright © Larousse plc 1994
Illustrations © George Buchanan 1994

A CIP catalogue record for this
book is available from the British Library

ISBN 1 85697 358 1

Phototypeset by Tracey McNerney
Printed in Spain
Designed by John Jamieson
Cover design by Terry Woodley

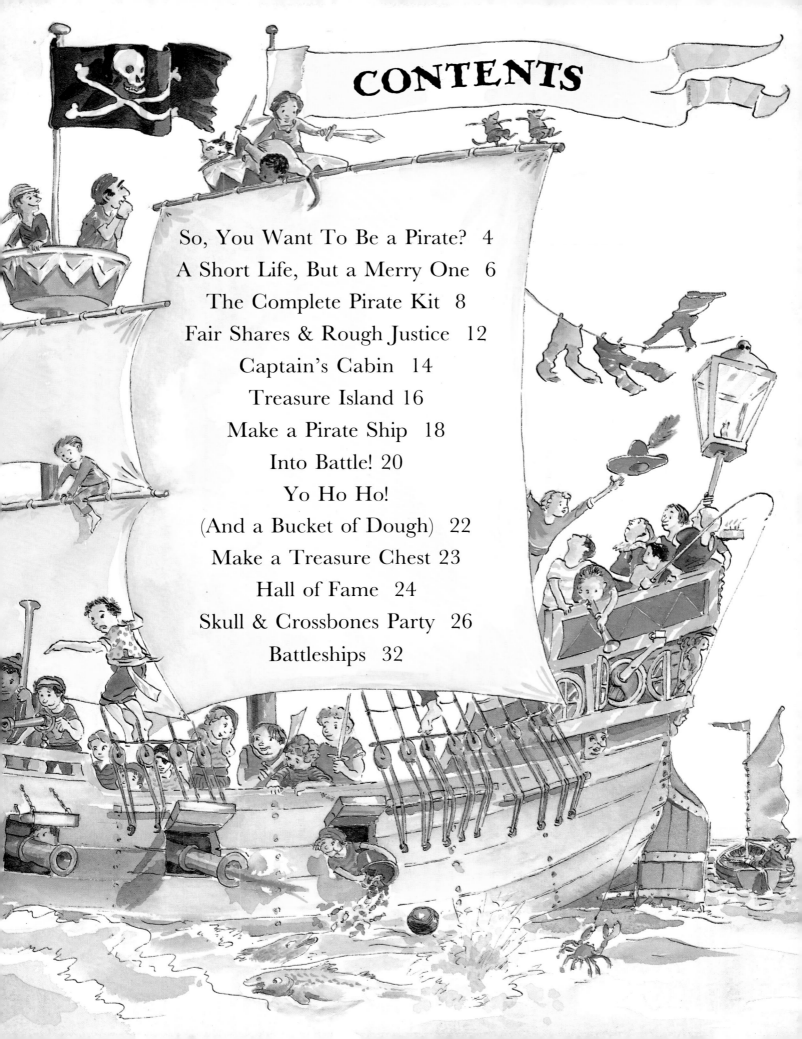

CONTENTS

SO, YOU WANT TO BE A PIRATE?

Have you ever longed to sail
the seven seas in search of thrills and adventure?
If so, why not become a pirate? In this book
you can read about some of the
wickedest pirates that ever lived.
You can also find out how to
make a hook, design a Jolly
Roger, build a pirate ship
and turn your bedroom
into a captain's cabin! All you
need is a basic kit like the one shown below.

WHAT YOU NEED

For most of the activities in this book, you'll need some
card, paper, paints, scissors and glue. Some of the
activities need special ingredients, such as flour,
split peas or a tea bag!

A COAT HANGER

OLD CEREAL BOXES

BRUSHES

SCISSORS

PENCILS

FELT-TIPPED PENS

STRING

POSTER PAINTS

THE SPANISH MAIN

Pirates have roamed the seas since ancient times, and some are still around today. But perhaps the most famous of all are the ones who sailed along the Spanish Main, about 300 years ago.

The Spanish Main was the name given to Central America, which Spain had invaded in the 1500s. Spanish soldiers stole all the gold and precious jewels that belonged to the Native Americans, and loaded it onto huge galleons to take back home. The pirates then robbed the Spanish galleons!

TREASURES FROM THE EAST

During the 1600s, the English often used pirates as a weapon in their war against Spain. Some pirates were even knighted for their efforts! However, once peace was made between the two countries, the laws against piracy toughened up. Many pirates headed for the Far East, where trading ships were returning to Europe laden with riches.

PIRATES AND PRIVATEERS

Real pirates robbed any ship they fancied, and kept the booty for themselves. Privateers, on the other hand, worked for their government. They carried special documents that allowed them to plunder any ship that belonged to the enemy.

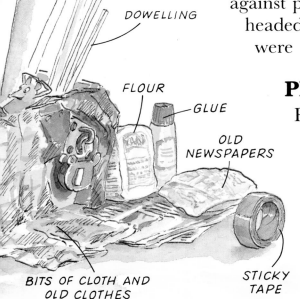

CARD AND PAPER

DOWELLING

FLOUR

GLUE

OLD NEWSPAPERS

BITS OF CLOTH AND OLD CLOTHES

STICKY TAPE

A SHORT LIFE, BUT A MERRY ONE

Being a pirate wasn't always exciting. Sometimes, whole months went by without anything happening at all!

In between raids, there were plenty of chores for the pirates to do. Musicians played jolly sea shanties to make the daily tasks go with a swing...

... and to help them wile away the long, moonlit evenings at sea.

Pirates spent a lot of their free time playing cards and dice. They also liked to dance and sing, and to drink rum and brandy – when they could get it!

The food was revolting. Meat and fish had to be smothered in salt to stop them going off. There were no fresh fruit or vegetables either, so the crew often went down with horrible illnesses such as scurvy.

Instead of bread, the pirates ate mouldy biscuits called 'hard tack'. These were often crawling with weevils after a few weeks at sea.

With a bit of luck, a pirate might be able to survive the food. However, he could still catch all kinds of ghastly diseases from the rats and bugs that scurried all over the ship...

The company on board a pirate ship was usually rough and dangerous. Some of the crew were thieves and murderers who had escaped from prison. Others had been mutineers, or had deserted from the army or the navy.

A pirate's life was full of risks and danger. If he wasn't killed during battle or poisoned by the food, he could easily end up in the hangman's noose! Although many captured pirates were pardoned, the ringleaders were usually hung for their crimes.

Many pirates had once been honest sailors, who had become fed up with harsh discipline and cruel captains. In many ways, life on board a pirate ship was a holiday after the navy!

But the main reason that men (and a few women) became pirates was the thought of getting rich quickly. Pirates could make more money out of one lucky raid than an honest sailor could earn in all his years at sea!

So, if the life was so hard and dangerous, why did people become pirates?

A lot of men ran away to sea to escape an even more miserable life on land. Some were fed up with the lack of jobs back home. Others had run away from jail, slave owners, or unhappy marriages!

FOR SALE

Even if they never managed to capture a treasure galleon, pirates could make a very good living from robbing small merchant ships of their cargo of cloth, spices, brandy and tobbacco, and selling it at the nearest port.

THE COMPLETE PIRATE KIT

Most pirates wore loose, baggy clothing that allowed them to move easily about the ship. Whenever they captured any well-dressed prisoners, they'd take the best clothing for themselves!

BASIC KIT

1 All you need is an old pair of trousers and a T-shirt – cut ragged edges with scissors, and add patches if you like.

2 Tie a scarf round your head – you could also sew a hoop earring or a curtain ring to the side. Or just tie the scarf around your neck.

3 Tie a big scarf round your waist, or buckle on a belt (you'll need this to hold your cutlass in place).

Pirates were always losing bits of themselves in battle. Here's how to make an eyepatch and a hook...

For the eyepatch, you will need: Some black paper; elastic; scissors; some glue

For the hook, you will need: A plastic bottle; scissors; a plastic coat hanger; some black emulsion paint

EYEPATCH

1 Cut a semi-circle from black paper, and fold over one edge.

2 Lay a piece of elastic along the crease, and glue down the edge. Tie the ends in a knot, making sure that it fits round your head comfortably.

HOOK

CUT A CROSS HERE

SNAP OFF HOOK

1 Cut the end off a plastic bottle. Cut a cross in the bottom.

2 Paint the bottle with black paint and leave it to dry.

3 Ask an adult to snap the hook off a plastic coat hanger.

4 Push the hook through the cross. Put your hand inside the bottle, and hold the broken end of the hook.

Captain's Kit

Many captains dressed in fine clothes – even during battle! Back in the 1600s, this meant a lot of ruffled shirts, fancy jackets and waistcoats, and some very large hats...

CAPTAIN'S CLOTHES

1 Sew shiny buttons onto a jacket. Add lace for extra glamour.

2 Tuck a pair of trousers into a pair of boots or wellingtons.

CAPTAIN'S HAT

You will need: Black card (about 45 x 40 cm); scissors; a stapler; white paint

1 Fold the card in half, and copy the pattern. Cut out both pieces, and staple the sides together.

2 Paint a skull and crossbones onto one side of the hat, using thick white poster paint.

20 cm

45 cm

CUT A FEATHER FROM PAPER, AND STAPLE TO HAT

PIRATE WEAPONS

To make these weapons, you will need: Some thick card; scissors; newspaper; wallpaper paste; poster paints; some clear polyurethane varnish

DAGGER

CUTLASS

8 cm

18 cm

15 cm

40 cm

1 Copy the cutlass and dagger onto thick card. Cut them out with scissors.

2 Mix up the paste, following the instructions given on the packet.

3 Tear several sheets of newspaper into small strips. Dip them into the paste, and smooth them over the weapons until they're covered. Leave to dry.

4 Repeat with two more layers. When dry, paint with silver and brown paint. Finish with a coat of varnish.

FAIR SHARES & ROUGH JUSTICE

Although pirates were ruthless thieves and murderers, they lived by a strict set of rules that they drew up themselves.

THE CAPTAIN

The ship was owned by the crew, and the crew elected the captain.

They obeyed him in battle, but at other times he could be outvoted – or even removed from his position!

THE RULES

All crew members had to sign a list of rules, called articles. If there wasn't a Bible handy, they swore to them on a hatchet!

All treasure, liquor and other gains were shared out equally among the crew – although the captain and his officers all got extra shares.

Any pirate caught striking a shipmate on board the ship would be flogged. All arguments had to be settled on land, when they reached port.

PIRATE PUNISHMENTS

Pirates were very hard on any shipmate who broke the rules.

Although walking the plank is such a well-known punishment, it probably never happened!

Marooning was a fate worse than death. The pirate was left on a deserted island, with only a gun, some shot and some water.

For small crimes, a pirate might be flogged with the 'cat o'nine tails' – a stick with nine pieces of knotted rope.

If a pirate was 'keel-hauled', he was dangled overboard, pulled under the ship, and scraped against the rough barnacles underneath.

Gambling for money was forbidden on board some ships.

For an eye or limb lost in battle, a pirate would receive an injury payment (for example, around £400 for a leg).

All weapons had to be kept clean and ready for service.

No women were allowed on board – though there were some exceptions to this rule!

CAPTAIN'S CABIN

Here's how to turn a corner of your own bedroom into a captain's cabin...

PORTHOLE

You will need:
Some card; a bin or saucepan lid; some split peas; scissors; glue; poster paints

1 Put the lid on the card. Draw around it, and cut out the shape.

2 Draw another circle inside the first one, to make the rim. Then glue split peas around the rim, to make 'rivets'.

TELESCOPE

You will need:
Three squares of thick paper, about 20 cm wide; paper-clips; scissors; glue; paints and brushes

1 Roll up a piece of card, and glue it down the side.

CLIPS HOLD TUBE TOGETHER WHILE GLUE DRIES

2 Roll up another piece. Push it into the first tube, and let go so that it fills the space.

LOGBOOK

You will need:
An exercise book with a stiff cover; some bits of card; string; glue; paints and brushes

1 Cut shapes from the card, and glue them onto the book.

ANCIENT MAP

You will need:
Thick white paper; a ball-point pen; a damp, used tea bag

1 Draw a map with the ball-point pen – you could trace a piece of coastline from an atlas, or invent your own.

3 Paint the rim gold or silver.

4 Paint a view in the middle!

'RIVETS'

3 Pull it out, and glue the sides.

4 Make a third tube. Then push the tubes back inside each other.

PAINT THE TELESCOPE

2 Coil pieces of string, and glue these on too.

3 Brush gold paint all over the book, and leave to dry. Then rub a little black paint along the edges of the card and string.

2 Press the tea bag all over the map. Try folding it up and tearing the edges, to make it look old.

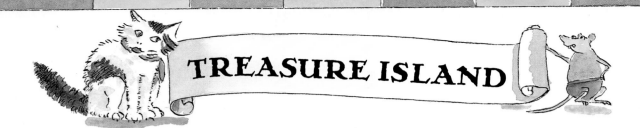

TREASURE ISLAND

Here's a treasure-hunting game for two,
three or four pirates to play. You'll need a dice,
and a coin or a button for each player.

FOULED ANCHOR. GO BACK TO SHIP.

CHASED BY CROCODILES! MOVE TO 10

RUN FOR YOUR LIFE! MOVE TO 14

MARCH ALL THROUGH THE NIGHT. HAVE ANOTHER GO.

FORGOT GROG AND VITTALS. GO GO BACK TO SHIP.

ROPE LADDER LOOKS UNSAFE. MISS A GO WHILE YOU FIX IT.

SLIP ON STEPPING STONES. SWIM TO RAFT.

THROW A 4, 5 OR 6 BEFORE MOVING TO 10

RAFT

THE RULES

1 Each player puts a coin on a ship (two or more players can choose the same ship, if they like).

2 Take turns to throw the dice, and move the number of spaces thrown. If you land on an anchor, carry out the instructions at the end of the chain.

3 Once on land, choose any path to get you to the treasure. When you've reached it (with an exact throw of the dice), make your way back to the ship. First back on board wins the game!

CHASED BY SNAKE! HAVE ANOTHER GO.

FALL INTO RIVER. SCRAMBLE OUT AT 13

FALL OFF LOG BRIDGE. MOVE TO 13

STOP TO ADMIRE STRANGE BIRD. MISS A GO.

BROKEN OARS. GO BACK TO SHIP.

PARROT FINDS SHORT CUT TO 15

CHASED BY WILD PIG. HAVE ANOTHER GO. (QUICKLY!)

ATTACKED BY LOCALS! RACE TO 13

MAKE A PIRATE SHIP

Pirate ships came in all shapes and sizes – quite a lot of them were stolen from their victims! Pirates liked the swift little merchant ships best of all. These were perfect for fast hit-and-run attacks.

You will need:
A cereal box;
sticky tape;
old newspapers;
wallpaper paste;
thin dowelling;
poster paints;
polyurethane
varnish; white
paper; cotton
thread

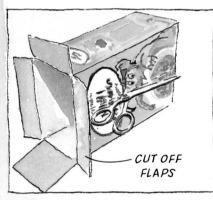

CUT OFF FLAPS

1 Cut the flaps off the box, and cut it in half lengthwise. Keep any spare card.

2 Cut the front and back of the box at a sloping angle, as shown above.

TAPE SIDES TOGETHER

FOLD UP AND TAPE

3 Curl up the two bottom flaps, and tape in place – you'll need to cut the front flap into a point to fit.

PRESS DOWN TO MAKE SIDES SPREAD OUT SLIGHTLY

DECK

TAPE DECK INSIDE BOAT

4 Turn the boat upside down on the spare card. Then draw around the shape, cut it out, and tape it inside the boat.

5 Mix up the paste, and tear the newspaper into small strips. Cover the boat with three layers (see page 11).

GUNWALE

GUNWALE

CANNON

MASTS

GLUE CANNONS
INSIDE GUNWALES

6 When dry, cut the 'gunwales' for the cannons (make these by rolling up some small pieces of paper, and holding them in place with tape).

BOWSPRIT

7 Cut two small crosses in the deck. Ask an adult to cut the dowelling into masts. Push these through the crosses, and glue in place.

8 Glue another piece of dowelling to the prow (the front of the ship), to make the bowsprit.

9 Paint your ship, and finish with a coat of varnish. Cut sails from paper or cotton, and tie them to the masts with the thread.
  Either cut pirate figures out of card, or use little toy pirates.

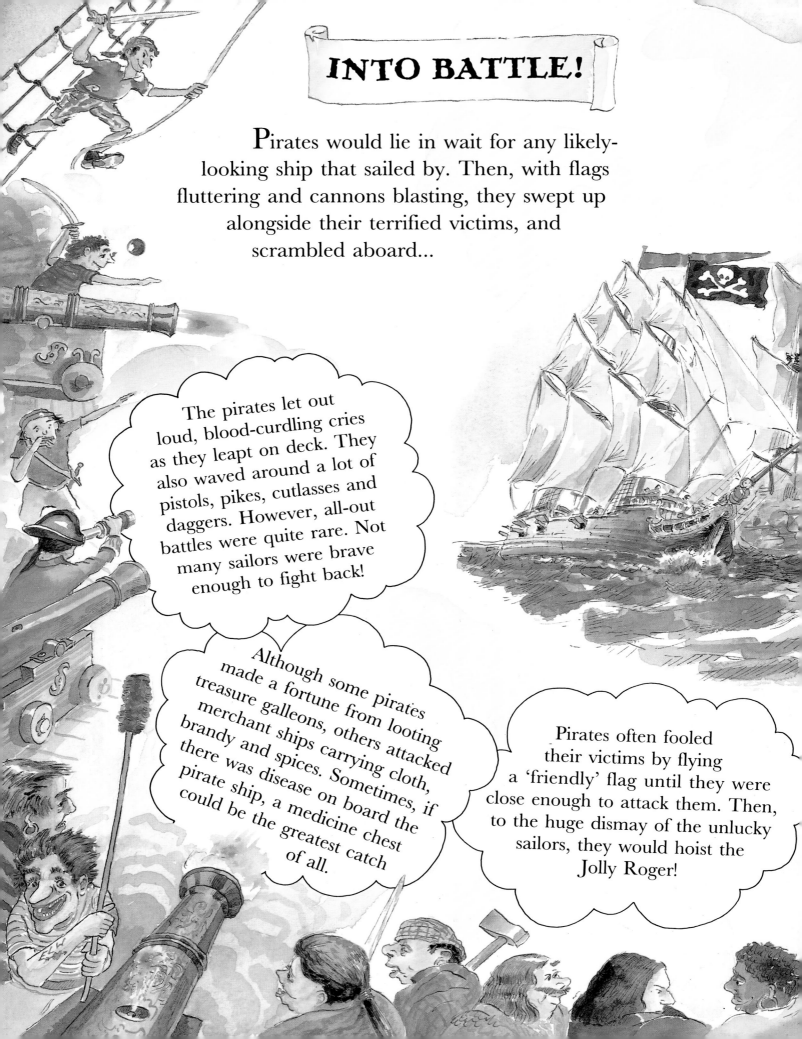

INTO BATTLE!

Pirates would lie in wait for any likely-looking ship that sailed by. Then, with flags fluttering and cannons blasting, they swept up alongside their terrified victims, and scrambled aboard...

The pirates let out loud, blood-curdling cries as they leapt on deck. They also waved around a lot of pistols, pikes, cutlasses and daggers. However, all-out battles were quite rare. Not many sailors were brave enough to fight back!

Although some pirates made a fortune from looting treasure galleons, others attacked merchant ships carrying cloth, brandy and spices. Sometimes, if there was disease on board the pirate ship, a medicine chest could be the greatest catch of all.

Pirates often fooled their victims by flying a 'friendly' flag until they were close enough to attack them. Then, to the huge dismay of the unlucky sailors, they would hoist the Jolly Roger!

The Jolly Roger

Many pirates flew a black flag with a spooky-looking skull and crossbone design. This was called the Jolly Roger, or Black Jack. Most pirate captains had their own flag, each with a slightly different pattern. Sometimes, they also hoisted a red flag. This meant that no mercy would be shown in battle.

To design a Jolly Roger, you will need: Some card; a pencil; scissors; white felt or paper; black felt or paper; glue; a stick

1 Sketch out a design for your own Jolly Roger on the piece of card.

2 Cut out your design. Draw round it onto white felt or paper, and cut out.

3 Cut a square of black paper or felt, and glue on the shapes. Glue a stick to the side.

YO HO HO! (AND A BUCKET OF DOUGH)

Yet another long evening at sea with nothing to do? Try making some salt-dough decorations for your cabin...

You will need:
225 g flour;
100 g salt;
150 ml water;
poster paints;
polyurethane varnish; kitchen foil; a knife

1 Sieve the flour into a bowl. Add the salt and water, and mix well until it makes a smooth dough.

2 Model as shown below. Then bake at 180°C/350°F/gas mark 4 for about 30 minutes. Leave to cool.

3 Paint, and when dry, give it a coat of varnish.

DOOR PLATE

ROLL OUT THE DOUGH UNTIL IT'S ABOUT 1cm THICK.

CUT A DOOR PLATE SHAPE, AND MAKE A HOLE AT EACH END FOR THE NAILS.

BAKE, AND PAINT WHEN COOL.

BEN'S CABIN

PIRATE ON A RAFT

ROLL BALLS AND SAUSAGES FROM DOUGH, TO MAKE PIRATE'S HEAD, BODY, ARMS AND LEGS.

PRESS FIVE SAUSAGES TOGETHER SIDE BY SIDE, TO MAKE THE RAFT.

PRESS DOUGH THROUGH A GARLIC PRESS TO MAKE HAIR!

MOULD CHEST, BARREL AND ANY OTHER BITS AND PIECES FROM DOUGH.

ASSEMBLE PIECES AND BAKE.

MAKE A
TREASURE CHEST

Right. You've become a highly successful pirate, and now need somewhere to stash all your ill-gotten gains. It's time to make a treasure chest...

You will need: a cardboard box; glue; sticky tape; paints; some split peas; polyurethane varnish; card

1 Cut the sides of the box, as shown in the picture.

2 Bend the back over. Try to make a smooth curve, *not* a sharp crease.

3 Cut the front bar, lock and bands from card. Fix these to the chest.

4 Cut four slits in the front. Cut two tabs from card, and fold as shown. Push the tabs through the slits, and tape inside.

FRONT BAR

LOCK

TAPE TO FRONT

GLUE ON SPLIT PEAS FOR 'RIVETS'

TAB

TAB

Paint and varnish the finished chest.

PIECES OF EIGHT

These were Spanish dollars (each dollar was worth eight 'reals'). Cut some from thick card – paint them silver, or cover in kitchen foil.

HALL OF FAME

Many pirates met a bloody death in battle, or were hung for their crimes. Others ended up with a knighthood!

Henry Morgan

No privateer ever led such a charmed life as Henry Morgan! His daring raids against the Spanish thrilled Charles II of England, who made him Deputy-Governor of Jamaica in 1674.

Captain Kidd

Kidd was hired to catch pirates for the government, but became a pirate himself. He was hung in 1701 – people have been searching for his treasure ever since.

Bartholomew Roberts

This interesting pirate captured no less than 400 ships. He was very religious, drank only tea, and liked his crew to be in bed by 8.00 pm sharp! Roberts was shot in battle in 1722.

MORGAN

KIDD

ROBERTS

Blackbeard

This alarming pirate liked to go into battle with burning fuses tied to his hair. Feared as much by his crew as he was by his enemies, Blackbeard was finally killed in 1718, by a young naval officer.

Anne Bonny & Mary Read

These hellcats of the high seas were the fiercest fighters on 'Calico Jack' Rackham's pirate ship. Unlike their captain, they were pardoned in 1720, and narrowly escaped the hangman's noose.

Francis Drake

Francis Drake was a famous English sea explorer and a popular hero in the 1500s. His reward for privateering was a knighthood from Queen Elizabeth I.

All but one of these pirates met their fate or made their fortune in and around the Spanish Main. Captain Kidd came unstuck in the Indian Ocean!

Why not throw a pirate party? Planning and making things is half the fun, especially if you ask a few shipmates to lend a hand...

PARROTS

Trace the parrot from page 32 onto card. Paint brightly, and cut out. Hang up with thread.

INVITATIONS

Make an eyepatch for each guest (see page 9), and send it to them along with the invitation.

YOU ARE INVITED TO A
SKULL & CROSSBONES PARTY
DATE .. OCTOBER 15th
PLACE .. SKULL ISLAND (TOM'S HOUSE)
TIME .. 3 PM ....
DRESS AS A PIRATE!
R.S.V.P. orelse!

USING MUSIC

Use music and other noises to help you set the mood. You should be able to borrow a tape of sailor's sea shanties, or sound effects of sailing ships from a library.

PALM TREES

Draw some bark segments and leaves onto card. Paint, cut out, and tape together at the back to make palm trees.

CROSSBONES PARTY

PLACE MARKERS

You will need: Thin card; tracing paper; paints and scissors

POLLY

1 Cut out a lot of rectangles from card – two for each guest. Draw lines across the middles.

2 Trace the shape from page 32 onto half the rectangles. Then cut out with some scissors, as shown.

3 Fold all the other rectangles in half. Then glue an island shape to the front of each rectangle.

27

Fun & Games

Here are some good games and activities for keeping your pirate guests out of trouble...

PIRATE PICTURES

You will need:
A roll of wallpaper lining; scissors; a pencil; plenty of paints and brushes

1 Cut several sheets of lining paper. Make each one a little bit longer than your own height.

2 As each guest arrives, pin one sheet to the wall and ask them to strike a piratical pose. Draw around them with a pencil.

FISHING

You will need:
Two rods or pencils; thread; two magnets; paper-clips; a bucket; some card; sticky tape; glue

1 Tie lengths of thread to the rods, and tie on the magnets. Then cut 20 fish, 15 pieces of eight, and 5 treasure chests from card.

2 Tape a paper-clip to each shape. Put a score on each one (e.g. 5 for a fish, 10 for each of the pieces of eight, and 25 for a chest).

BLACK SPOT

Give each player two circles cut from black paper, and get them all to stand in line. Then shout GO!

1 Each pirate puts a spot down and stands on it with one foot. He or she then puts the next spot down, and stands on it with the other foot.

TREASURE ISLAND

You will need:
A sheet of polystyrene; paper; some paints; cocktail sticks

1 Paint an island on the paper, and tape it to the polystyrene. Put an X under the paper. Cut a paper flag for each pirate, and glue to the cocktail sticks.

3 The guests then use paint to turn their outlines into fierce pirates!

PUT DOWN PLENTY OF NEWSPAPER!

Make a hat for each pirate (see page 10), and ask them to paint on their own design.

3 Put all the shapes in the bucket, and divide the pirates into two teams.

25 25

4 A pirate from each team fishes until they get a catch. Then two others have a go.

5 When the bucket is empty, count up the score. Award the winners a bag of chocolate coins!

2 The pirate then lifts his or her foot off the first spot, picks the spot up, puts it in front, and steps on it!

3 See who can reach the finish line first – anyone who puts their foot on the ground and not on a spot is disqualified!

2 Ask each pirate to stick their flag on the island. Then check whose flag is nearest the X!

HANNAH LEILA GEORGE ALEX

29

Grog & Vittals (Drink & Food)

Luckily for your guests, the food at your party will taste about a million times better than anything the real pirates had for tea! Follow the ideas and recipes shown below.

LEMONADE

(to protect against scurvy)

You will need:
6 lemons
100 g caster sugar
180 ml water

1 Grate the lemon rind. Put it in a heatproof jug, along with the sugar.

2 Boil the water, and pour it into the jug. Stir until the sugar dissolves.

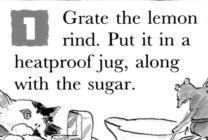

NECKLACES

Cut cotton into 35-cm lengths. Use a darning needle to thread on chunks of cheese, apple and pineapple; hula hoops; grapes; pretzels; cooked sausages, etc.

CANNONBALLS

(for pirates with a sweet tooth)

TREASURE CHESTS

You will need:
A chocolate mini-roll for each guest
Colourful small sweets (such as jelly beans or smarties)

Cut each mini-roll in half. Put a few sweets inside, and replace the top!

HARD TACK

Buy some chocolate chip cookies, and pretend the chips are weevils!

3 Squeeze the lemons, and pour into the jug through a sieve. Serve chilled.

PIRATE BOATS

Just split some bread rolls in half, spread with butter and top with some of your favourite fillings.

Use paper and some cocktail sticks to make sails and masts!

For about 20 cannonballs, you will need:
100 g soft cheese
100 g chopped walnuts
100 g icing sugar
50 g cocoa powder
Some drinking chocolate powder

1 Stir the cheese, nuts, cocoa and sugar together until well mixed.

2 Roll the mixture into small balls, each the size of a walnut. Roll each ball in chocolate powder, and put in tiny paper cases.

JELLY BOATS

For 24 boats, you need:
6 large oranges
2 packets of jelly

1 Cut each orange in half.

2 Scoop out all the flesh. Then make up the jelly. Follow the instructions on the packet, but use a little less water.

3 Pour the jelly into the orange halves, and put in the fridge. When set, cut each one in half.

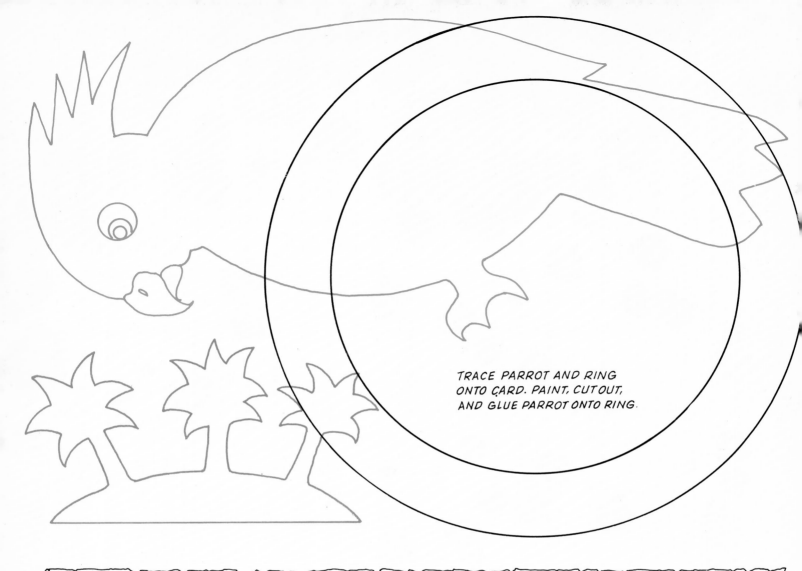

TRACE PARROT AND RING
ONTO CARD. PAINT, CUT OUT,
AND GLUE PARROT ONTO RING.

Battleships

To play this game, you'll need some paper, pencils, and another pirate. First, draw a grid like the one here. Number the squares 1-13 along the top, and write the letters A-M down the side.

1 Pirate 1 secretly marks 20 ships on his map, while pirate 2 marks 20 ships on hers.

then calls out a grid reference. If she 'hits' a ship on pirate 1's map, he crosses it off.

2 Pirate 1 calls out a grid reference – e.g. B2. If pirate 2 has a ship on this square, she must cross this off. Pirate 2

3 The first pirate to sink all of the enemy's ships wins the game!